Poems about

Families

Selected by
Amanda Earl & Danielle Sensier

Illustrated by
Frances Lloyd

Wayland

Titles in the series
Poems about . . .

Animals	**Food**
Colours	**Growth**
Day & Night	**Homes**
Families	**Journeys**
Feelings	**Weather**

For Mum and Dad

Series editor: Catherine Baxter
Designer: Loraine Hayes

First published in 1994 by
Wayland (Publishers) Ltd
61 Western Road, Hove
East Sussex BN3 1JD, England

Typeset by Dorchester Typesetting
Group Ltd., Dorset, England.
Printed and bound in Italy by
G. Canale & C.S.p.A., Turin.

British Library Cataloguing in Publication Data

Poems About Families. – (Poems About . . .
Series)
I. Earl, Amanda II. Sensier, Danielle
III. Series
821.008
ISBN 0-7502-1123-7

Front cover design S. Balley

Poets' nationalities

Tony Bradman	English
Sarah Day	English
Max Fatchen	Australian
Brian Patten	English
Colin McNaughton	English
Judith Viorst	American
Christina Rossetti	English/Italian
Micheal Xenofontos	Greek Cypriot
Grace Nichols	Guyanese
Mick Gowar	English

Contents

I Wish

I wish I was
An only child
No brothers or sisters
To drive me wild

> I wish I had
> An older brother
> And a sister
> And another

I hate it when
We have a fight
I'm always wrong
They're always right

> I hate it when
> There's no one there
> To play with me
> To laugh, to share

Tony Bradman

4

Me And My Bruv

Me and my bruv get along just great,
My bruv's twelve and I'm nearly eight;
We support United, my bruv and me,
And clock all the football on the TV.
My bruv's at big school, he does French and Maths;
When I show him my News, my bruv laughs.
We like beef-burglars, oven chips and peas,
That's me and my bruv's favourite teas.
We don't like homework, my bruv gets tons;
Even my bruv can't do my sums.
My bruv collects things, real antiques,
And tapes and comics, he's got heaps.
Bruv's into software, that means games;
Doing the computer really takes brains.
Our mum says my bruv's a big lazy lump,
And me and my bruv's room's a rubbish dump.
It's half his mess, but he blames me, still –
I luv my bruv, my bruv's mega-brill!

Stephen Mulrine

Our Family

Sue works in a shop. John's driving a
  bus,
Joan's married to Frank and is not
  living with us,
Tom wants to leave school as soon as he
  can,
Father still speaks like a west
  countryman;
So that's all of us, with Mother and me,
In our family.

Crystella's from Cyprus, George, Port of
  Spain,
His father talks cricket and works on a
  crane,
Lynn, born in Jamaica, is slender and
  tall,
Fazi wears earrings and comes from
  Bengal;
So that's some of them, their mothers,
  and me,
In our family.

Leonard Clark

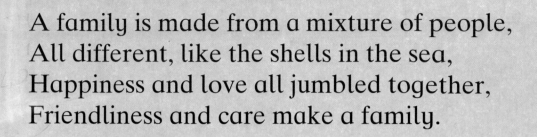

A family is made from a mixture of people,
All different, like the shells in the sea,
Happiness and love all jumbled together,
Friendliness and care make a family.

Sarah Day (aged 12)

Control Calling

Just when I am conducting
A manoeuvre tactical
On my spaceship galactical,
Using my unidentified-object locators,
With my forward disintegrators
Whamming and shooting,
And my astro-clad officers saluting
Amid the rocketry's swirls and swishes,
My sister Kate
Cries 'Activate'
And I'm back on earth,
Drying dishes.

Max Fatchen

10

This is the Mum

This is the mum
Who wakes me up
And gets me out of bed

This is the mum
Who helps me pull
My clean vest over my head

This is the mum
Who irons my clothes
Who puts out my clean socks

This is the mum
Who puts my lunch
Inside my new lunchbox

This is the mum
Who goes to work
Who tries not to be late

This is the mum
Who stands in the rain
By the infant gate

Tony Bradman

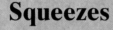

Squeezes

We love to squeeze bananas,
We love to squeeze ripe plums,
And when they are feeling sad
We love to squeeze our mums.

Brian Patten

Mum Is Having A Baby!

Mum is having a baby!
  I'm shocked! I'm all at sea!
What's she want another one for:
  WHAT'S THE MATTER WITH ME!?

Colin McNaughton

Some things don't make any sense at all

My mum says I'm her sugarplum.
My mum says I'm her lamb.
My mum says I'm completely perfect
Just the way I am.
My mum says I'm a super-special wonderful terrific little guy.
My mum just had another baby.
Why?

Judith Viorst

Fred

I haven't got a dad.
But I'm not sad.
I live with my mum.
My mum's got a boyfriend
– he's real good fun.
His name is Fred.
He drives a lorry.
The lorry's red.
He takes me with him:
we bomb down the road,
we go to a caff,
and then we unload.
He calls me his mate.
I think Fred's great.

Nigel Gray

Two in bed

When my brother Tommy
Sleeps in bed with me,
He doubles up
And makes
himself
exactly
like
a
V
And 'cause the bed is not so wide,
A part of him is on my side.

A. B. Ross

brilliant – like me

today I went with Mum
and Dad on the bus and
the train for our baby

it took us three hours
to travel all that way
but we knew she'd be
worth the long journey

our baby and me are
adopted, but we both
have freckly skin
and I laughed today
when I saw her – she
gave me a gummy grin

I laughed when I saw
her – looking just
like me, she's even got
a funny pointy chin

I'm glad Mum and Dad
chose our baby – I'm
glad they both chose me
it's going to be great
to have a little sister

I think she's brilliant
like me.

Joan Poulson

Motherless Baby

Motherless baby and babyless mother,
Bring them together to love one another.

Christina Rossetti

18

Grandad's Hands

Grandad's got two big, kind hands,
One for Chrissie and one for me,
If we had another
Sister or brother,
God would have given him three.

Jean Willis

My Grandfather in Cyprus

I'd like to meet my grandad
But he lives in a land far away,
Where it is hot and sunny.
I hear he is an old man now,
His face is wrinkled like a lemon in the sun.
When we meet
We will talk in Greek,
Someday.

Micheal Xenofontos

from **Mama, Papa and Baby Joe**

Under over Coca-Cola
Off to Pick 'n' Pay we go,
Moany moany macaroni,
Mama, Papa, and Baby Joe.

Harum-scarum through the traffic
Ziggery-zaggery park the car.
Bumpity-bump along the pavement
Around the block and there you are!

In and out the shops so busy
Mama and Papa go yakety-yak.
See you later, escalator
Okeydokey, clickety-clack . . .

Spaghetti falling pitter-pat,
Hot and bothered screaming Mama
'DON'T DO THAT!' **'DON'T DO THAT!'**

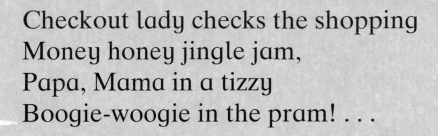

Checkout lady checks the shopping
Money honey jingle jam,
Papa, Mama in a tizzy
Boogie-woogie in the pram! . . .

In Fatty Boom Boom's Take Away,
Sticky icky licking baby
Mama smiling, it's OK! . . .

Shopping packed and home we go!
Honky-tonky through the city
Mama, Papa, and sleepy Joe.

Niki Daly

Granny Granny Please Comb my Hair

Granny Granny please comb
my hair
you always take your time
you always take such care

You put me on a cushion
between your knees
you rub a little coconut oil
parting gentle as a breeze

Mummy Mummy
she's always in a hurry-hurry
rush
she pulls my hair
sometimes she tugs

But Granny
you have all the time
in the world
and when you're finished
you always turn my head and say
'Now who's a nice girl'

Grace Nichols

Daddy

Daddy lives in Tate Street now
he's got a flat
with patchy orange walls
and grey armchairs that
smell of someone else
And every Saturday we sleep there
Jo and me

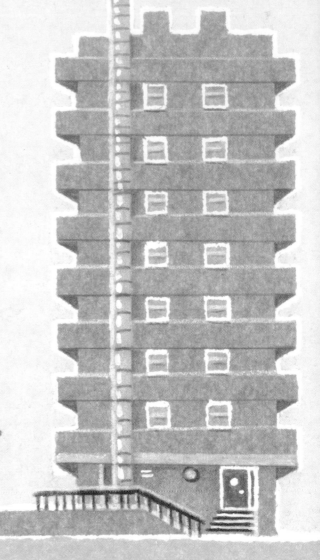

Daddy lives in Tate Street now
he's got a flat
it's up a winding flight of stairs
it's cold and
dark at night it feels as though there's
no one there
not even Daddy Jo and me

Daddy lives in Tate Street now
he's got a flat
he grows tomatoes in a pot outside
and in a week or two
we'll help him put them on
a windowsill to ripen
Daddy says

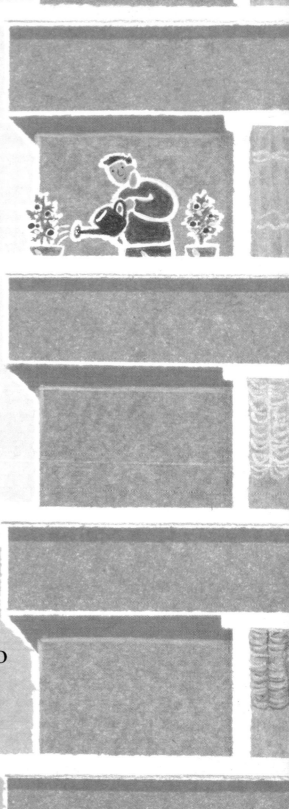

Daddy lives in Tate Street now
he's got a flat
and we go out a lot
to films and fairs and
Christmas time he'll take us to
A Pantomime
he's promised

Daddy lives in Tate Street now
hc's got a flat
he takes us home on Sunday
Mummy's in the kitchen Dick's there too
He's cooking something
Daddy says Goodbye
                    and then
goes home

Mick Gowar

Eskimo Lullaby

It's my fat baby
I feel in my hood.
Oh, how heavy he is!

When I turn my head
he smiles at me, my baby,
Hidden in my hood,
Oh, how heavy he is!

How pretty he is when he smiles
With his two teeth, like a little walrus!
and my hood full!

Anonymous (from Greenland)

How to use this book

Poetry is a very enjoyable area of literature and children take to it naturally, usually beginning with nursery rhymes. It's what happens next that can make all the difference! This series of thematic poetry anthologies keeps poetry alive and enjoyable for young children.

When using these books there are several ways in which you can help a child to appreciate poetry and to understand the ways in which words can be carefully chosen and sculpted to convey different atmospheres and meanings. Try to encourage the following:

- Joining in when the poem is read out loud.
- Talking about favourite words, phrases or images.
- Discussing the illustration and photographs.
- Miming facial expressions to suit the mood of the poems.
- Acting out events in the poems.
- Copying out the words.
- Learning favourite poems by heart.
- Discussing the difference between a poem and a story.
- Clapping hands to rhythmic poems.
- Talking about metaphors/similes eg what kind of weather would a lion be? What colour would sadness be? What would it taste like? If you could hold it, how would it feel?

It is inevitable that, at some point, children will want to write poems themselves. Writing a poem is, however, only one way of enjoying poetry. With the above activities, children can be encouraged to appreciate and delight in this unique form of communication.

Picture acknowledgements

Ace 11 (Anders Kustas), 17 (Mark Stevenson); Cephas 6 (P A Broadbent); Frank Lane 20 (Michael Clark), 29 (E & D Hosking); Impact 5 (Simon Shepheard), 19 (Rupert Conant); Life File cover (Nicola Sutton), 16 (Arthur Jumper); Robert Harding 25 (Adam Woolfitt); Tony Stone Worldwide (Ken Fisher), 14.

Text acknowledgements

For permission to reprint copyright material the publishers gratefully acknowledge the following: Curtis Brown for 'Grany Granny Please Comb My Hair' by Grace Nichols. Reprinted by permission of Curtis Brown Group Ltd London on behalf of Grace Nichols. Copyright © Grace Nichols, 1984; Nigel Gray for 'Fred'. Reprinted by permission of the author; John Johnson Limited for 'Control Calling' by Max Fatchen. Reprinted by permission of John Johnson Limited (Author's Agents); Stephen Mulrine for 'Me and My Bruv'. Reprinted by permission of the author; Brian Patten for 'Squeezes'. Reprinted by permission of the author; Random House UK Ltd for 'Grandad's Hands' from *'Toffee Pockets'* by Jean Willis. 'Mama, Papa and Baby Joe', from *'Mama, Papa and Baby Joe'*, by Niki Daly. Published by The Bodley Head. Reprinted by permission of Random House UK Ltd; Scholastic Publications Ltd for 'I'm Carrying the Baby' from *'Don't Put Mustard in the Custard'* by Michael Rosen. Reprinted by permission of Scholastic Publications Ltd; Walker Books for 'Mum Is Having a Baby' from *'Who's Been Sleeping in My Porridge'* by Colin McNaughton. Reprinted by permission of Walker Books. While every effort has been made to secure permission, in some cases it has proved impossible to trace the copyright holders. The publishers apologise for this apparent negligence.

Index of first lines